Randy,

all the best!

Growing Up
Irish

Eileen A. Canning

Eileen A. Canning

DEDICATION

I dedicate this book to my parents who came to America from the west
coast of Ireland, adopted me and gave me an awesome childhood. I am
eternally grateful for everything they have done and given me.
And to all their Irish family and friends, both living and gone, I raise a
glass in their honor.

CONTENTS

Acknowledgments   i

1   I Want a Blonde Baby Girl   Pg # 1

2   The Stone Wall of Glenfarne   Pg # 4

3   Dad's County Mayo   Pg # 22

4   The Keavenys and McTernans "One of a Kinds"   Pg # 33

5   My Comical, Yet Steadfast Irish Parents   Pg # 39

6   Interesting Places in Ireland   Pg # 56

7   Odd Sod Stories

    (Strange and Unique Stories from the Old Sod Herself)   Pg # 63

8   Superstitions, Beliefs and Samhain   Pg # 74

9   Influence of the Celtic Goddess   Pg # 76

10   My Journey Continues…   Pg # 79

    About the Author   Pg # 88

ACKNOWLEDGMENTS

To the story tellers and Irish historians, I acknowledge you with this book.
My wish is that this book will help me stay connected to my Irish lineage
and all the relatives who have gone on to the next phase of life.
Stories are an important part of Celtic history. I hope that those included
in this book will teach and inspire all who read it.

I WANT A BLONDE BABY GIRL

That was exactly what mom had said. She told me so later in my adult life. I was six months old when my adopted parents brought me home.

I was adopted from Father Baker's in Lackawanna, New York, at least that is what my birth certificate says. I had another name before my parents gave me the name I have now but it was never clear as to what that name was. My parents already had a son, they adopted him two years earlier.

When I was little, I couldn't understand why I didn't look like anyone else in my family. And in third grade, I was excused from doing a special project the teacher called a 'family tree' because I was told, it would have caused some serious confusion. The teacher knew I was adopted and made me feel that being adopted was like having some sort of disease because I had to sit out of that classroom project and didn't know why. I didn't know what "adopted" meant at the time and I felt I wasn't normal like the rest of my classmates. It was never explained to me.

And it's funny, because if you are 100% Irish, or even a little bit, you might already feel that you are different. I don't mean 'different' in a bizarre sort of way but sometimes things just might be, well, you know - different.

One of the first memories I have of coming home with my Irish parents is seeing a yellowish kind of light shining above my head. I think one of my parents must have been carrying me up our driveway and I saw the kitchen light over the sink shining through the window.

They brought me home at Samhain (in America it is called Halloween).

Now, if you know your Irish history and such, you'll remember that Samhain, ie. Halloween, came from Ireland. Samhain, (Sow-when or Som-ven) is celebrated at the end of October and beginning of November. It is a special day to honor the spirits of deceased ancestors. So what an interesting time to bring me home! I got a new life with Irish parents at Samhain.

Now, Halloween is something quite different from Samhain. The sacred aspects of it were left behind when the Western World adopted it. There will be more on this later on since I really should get back to the whole adoption story.

One of the interesting tidbits is that my mom was looking for a blonde baby girl. She had her heart set on finding one and she got me. She got ME!

I grew up feeling a bit confused about the relationship I had with my cousins and such but I learned to adapt to most of the family situations that were awkward. Sometimes I felt that some of the cousins pushed me and my brother away a little maybe they knew we were not the real children of my parents but later on it didn't matter to me so much. We fit in at home and that was that.

So what is this book about then? It's about growing up with Irish parents and the funny stories about their thick, Irish accents. It's about taking trips to the Emerald Isle to bring in the harvest hay for the winter months. There are stories about "Mommy Travers" as well as tales of old stone circles and ancient ancestors. It's a tribute to the ways of my late Irish parents, the ones who allowed me to adopt them.

Céad Míle Fáilte! (A hundred-thousand welcomes!)

Mom and dad and their Aran wool sweaters.

Growing Up Irish

THE STONE WALL OF GLENFARNE

My cousin Aidan, Rex the dog, me, my cousin Nuala

My mom and maternal grandmother grew up in Glenfarne in County Leitrim, Ireland. Their land consisted of several acres of land, a three bedroom cottage with a main seating area, an outhouse, a separate stone house for chickens, and two other nearby small stone cottages or out buildings. One of those dwellings was where the donkey was kept and the other was where Uncle Peter milked the cow.

There was an orchard on their farmland and two shallow creeks. The one furthest from the house had a waterfall that the boys would climb up when they were younger. I always wanted to join them but was too little to get to the top.

The creek closest to the house had a two and a half inch thick reddish stone slab bridge that you could walk across. The water was not very deep and it flowed downhill. It was the genius idea of a previous family member to build the outhouse on that creek so that all the deposits flowed downhill as well. Now, I know that many folks find outhouses a thing of the past but we had one and I got to use it. For me it was just a normal part of visiting grandma. It was there and it was where you 'went', when you had to well you know, *go*. Anyhow, this outhouse was at the end of a path that we walked down and it didn't have any lighting, so it really was a 'man vs. nature' kind of event.

I recall a particular time when it was dark outside and my mom had to pee so she showed me an alternative to using the outhouse on the creek bed. She demonstrated the most amazing squat, balanced herself very carefully on the reddish stone slab and 'went.' She mastered this squatting down bit and I was truly amazed that my six foot tall mother could do this with such grace. I tried not to think of it but if she ever tipped over, I would have had to run and get one of the bigger kids or even Uncle Peter to fish her out of the creek bed. But she never fell in thank goodness and I was able to master the mighty squat for myself when it was too dark to walk down the wooded path. We had chamber pots for during the night, but you didn't want to use it unless you really had to 'cause you might have had to smell it all night, even though it was tucked under the bed.

Now, there is more thing I wish to say about the wonderful wooden box on the creek bed and I promise I will move on to the next subject matter. You were expected to use the outhouse during the daylight because it was just not proper to let everyone, especially the boys, see you doing your 'business' squatting on the bridge during the daytime.

But, here's the thing, I hate spiders and there were always plenty of them hanging about in the loo (the toilet) and at any moment, one could show up on the door handle or come down from the rickety boards above. Not knowing if a spider would show itself, I decided to leave the door open. If I saw one I could bolt. As I groped around in the dimly lit interior for the roll of toilet paper I kept an all watching eye towards the opening in the door. One of the boys, or maybe even my brother, might just decide to peek or play a mean joke by locking me up in there. While watching toward the door and keeping an eye out for spiders something much more frightening caught the corner of my eye. Something white, tall and silent was floating through the trees. Did I just see a ghost? At that moment I fulfilled every child's dream of flying while breaking the hinge from the door. I ran so fast up the little inclined path, smashed through the gate and tore into the house. After convincing absolutely no one for a half an hour that I had seen a ghost I was put to bed, alone. I stared at the ceiling and the shadows on the walls. I remember too that there was a creepy looking chair in the corner facing the bed. I played the scene over and over in my head. The family's dog Rex had run away a few weeks earlier so maybe it was him returning to his loving home or maybe one of the cows was loose and walking upright. It made more sense to my young mind that I had really seen a ghost, because I knew for sure that cows could not walk on two legs and what I saw was several feet tall, white and moved very quietly. This was my first encounter with something that could not be explained by the family.

There was a wall made of round stones on the right hand side of the old thatched house. It was one of the boundary markers of the front yard. There were a few level stone slabs on the ground leading from the side entrance gate to the only door of the cottage. Next to the stone slabs, the rest of the front yard was grass, mud and clay. It was dry and flat unless it rained. If it was wet, it was slippery and then everyone would grab their wellingtons (also known as wellies) so they wouldn't slip or get mud on their shoes.

I wrote the following in honor of the approach to the old Irish cottage. My mom would scorn me, saying things like, *'don't cha be tellin' people 'bout 'dat ould house,'* and *'stop glorifyin' that ol' place.'* But all I was doing was loving the quaintness of it all.

> I used to brag to grade school friends about my family owning the longest driveway. It was also known as a road and it was off the old main route in Glenfarne, Ireland. As the car climbed that winding driveway, three stops had to be made so a passenger (usually a child) could hop out and open a series of gates. They were there to keep the cows and the bull from going where they

were not supposed to go.

I always looked forward to seeing the magnificent stone wall. It was on the right side of the house. Large round stones created the long, three foot high masterpiece. The cousins would challenge each other and us to see who could run and jump over the wall in a single leap. Sometimes, mice scurried through its tiny cracks while other small animals used its crevices for shelter during thunderstorms.

And where the stone wall ended, the little white post was mounted. It was a dainty thing, not designed to keep out intruders because there was nothing to be kept out then except for the milking cow and she would only come into the yard when Uncle Peter missed her milking time. The small white post held a companion on its hinge. A swinging gate was its best friend and even though the top hinge was bent back from the little ones rushing through it, the two held fast together. It was just enough to present a charming entranceway that led to the careworn cottage door. I remember sitting on the stone wall, laughing and singing while enjoying the harvest fires. I used to push my feet against the gate and watch it swing open and close.

Many dances were held inside the humbled yard of clay and pebble-stone and the half-hinged gate squeaked of its own melody as it played in time with the trooping dancers. In my kindest dreams, my spirit carries me back to that winding driveway. To satisfy my heart's longing it returns me to that stone wall, the open yard it kept, and the white fence with its off-set companion swinging in the breeze. Upwards it carries me, to that gentle entrance and the tiny cottage so careworn and overgrown. Yet, even in my dreams I recognize every green shrub, yellow wildflower and the uneven grooves of the pathway that led to the charming front door. In my dreams, I own it all again.

But on my last visit to Glenfarne, I was sad because the entire wall had been stolen away, perhaps to build a memory for another little white fence.

Yet in my mind, the wall and gate are still hinged together. Maybe someday the two companions will reunite. I pray that the memory of what I once had will allow me to make a new heaven, in a place that shelters its reflection.

Uncle Peter, two of his sons, a kitten and the white gate.

The road or driveway up to the cottage was indeed very long and there were big swinging gates that had to be opened on the way up. My cousins must have thought I was crazy because I loved to be the one to open the gates every time the car drove up the road.

They used a field rotation system so the grass that was eaten by the cows had a chance to grow back. I remember they had four separate green fields so each field had three years to grow back. These fields were protected behind those gates and the cows could not get to them unless someone mistakenly left one of the gates open.

The house, as it looked on one of my last visits.

The stone wall once ran alongside the edge of the front yard here. The gate and poles holding it in place were removed as well. The roof was caving in the last time I visited the old cottage. The building at the back was used as a chicken coup. There was a shallow creek that ran at the far end of the cottage with the family's outhouse just down the way in a wooded area. I remember another small white gate that had to be passed through on the way to the loo.

Getting back to the stone wall, I remember climbing on it in order to get onto the back of the family's donkey. He was a sweet grey thing, had huge teeth and would crunch very loudly when you fed him slices of bread. I used to sneak food out to him in his shed because I enjoyed feeding him. I remember they kept him in a separate little house of his own near the fruit orchard. We rode on him inside that stone wall all around within the enclosed yard. Sometimes there were as many as four of us small children sitting on him at one time. I don't think he minded so much, he was an easy going fellow. I also believe he was quite content knowing that one little girl was going to sneak him a treat later on.

I also remember Uncle Peter's cow wandering into the front yard on occasion. She came right up to the cottage door. Her big swollen belly swung to and fro and she got everybody's attention by mooing quite loudly. It was as if she was coming to tell Uncle Peter that he must have forgotten about her milking time. Like the donkey, she was very friendly.

I recall Peter squirting me with her udders once when I went to spy on them in the small stone structure where he was milking her. We used to drink her milk too. Uncle Peter would milk her, run the milk through a sieve and that was it. It tasted pretty good too. It seemed to be creamier and thicker than the watered-down milk today. I truly believe that it just tasted better then. We also made our own butter using the cream from the milked cow.

I am in the middle here surrounded by a few of my cousins.

Another little activity I participated in inside the stone wall was washing clothes. The family had an old washing machine that had a ringer on the top of it. Someone would hand-crank the clothes in order for them to be rung out. They wheeled this contraption out onto the stone walkway so that the splashing water would not get all over the floor inside the cottage.

The house itself was plain but what we did and how we entertained ourselves was how we lived there and that was that. We also, on occasion, went out to the field to gather turf for the stove.

This photo was taken while standing next to the chicken coup. The cow's milking house is on the left. The house is through the nook to the right.

My mom with the 'bug' and the outbuildings behind her.

My grandmother on the left here with one of the family's dogs. Mom, Aunt Kathleen and two of the children.

**One of my cousins with a lamb. The chicken coup
is in the back, the cow's milking house to the right.**

**My brother Tom and one of the cousins
in the tractor at Glenfarne.**

My mother and her siblings attended Cullentra School. I have a picture
from a reunion that took place in the late 1980's. I'm sure that the long,
arduous walk to the school must have been uphill both ways. There was
quite a long distance between the cottage and the old school and I know for
myself that the long 'driveway' down to the main thoroughfare was a hike
in itself.

Using a social media site in 2015, with the help of Mark Fitzpatrick, several of these fine folks were given a name when I posted this photo. The mystery was solved when I finally learned who the relative was. The first woman in the front row on the left was my mom's youngest sister Annie. She was my mom's favorite sister.

Back ; Phelim Byrne, Peter McMorrrow, John J McLoughlin(brother of Mrs Slevin), Sean McPartlin, Norman Elliott, John P McMorrow, Mary McManus (sister of Felix), James Clancy, Bridie McManus (sis of Felix), Patrick J.Healy, George Elliott, Felix McManus and Michael McLoughlin (brother of Mrs Slevin)

Middle ; Mrs Slevin, Larry Keaney, Maura (McPartlan) McSharry, Mary Kate McLoughlin, Mary Alice Healy, Betty Elliott

Front: Patty Byrne, Rosaleen Travers, Annie Travers, Patty Cullen, Master Cunningham, Annie Kate McLoughlin,Kathleen (Healy) McDermott and Anna Josephine (Healy) Ferguson.

My maternal grandmother, mom and all her siblings.

My mom was one of nine children and this is how I knew them. There was Annie, Sissy, Baby, Margaret, Kathleen, John Francis, Peter and Jimmy. Mom's mother was nick-named "Mommy-Travers" and that was what my cousins, her own children and I called her. Everyone had a high level of respect for her. She was the head of the household at Glenfarne and when I visited there, it was definitely her place. Uncle Peter, his wife and their six children all shared that thatched roof dwelling with her, but she was definitely at the helm.

In the Land of Tir Na NÓg, inhabitants live forever. "Mommy Travers" aka Grandmother, from the O'Hara Clan, lived to be 100 and according to her own view, it was long enough. Born in 1892, my mother's mom was the matriarch of the Travers' household in Manorhamilton. In fact, I believe she was the matriarch of the entire county.

"Mommy-Travers" with her husband.

My own mother, Frances, a.k.a. Jo, was the 'Matriarch of Wabash Avenue' in Kenmore, NY. She ruled the entire neighborhood with her shouts of accented commands and laughter. Like her mother, she passed away in December. Grandma died on Christmas morning, mom passed into the light on the ninth. She created a legacy of insight, power and humor and passed it on to me before leaving her human world.

Glenfarne

For the longest time, they seemed to have the same four chickens on the old farm in Glenfarne and that one milking cow I spoke of earlier. They had the donkey in my younger years and the blue bull as well. I have photos of the blue bull, but since this book is printed in black and white, the picture will not do him justice. My younger cousin, Nuala always said that this particular bull was 'cross.' This meant he was mean and that one should avoid getting him angry if they wanted to walk through his grazing area. There was one particular time when he is said to have chased one of my cousins through the field. I guess they lost their footing on cow droppings and landed in a fresh pile while trying to escape the chase. I guess that's how she learned that he was indeed, cross. I was grateful for the warning. A picture of him is included here and he is indeed an odd sort. I've never seen a bull with horns *and* an udder!

The blue bull.

We mostly visited the family in early fall and on a few occasions, I made my school teachers angry when I missed the first few weeks of school.

When I was about eight years old I had the fun experience of harvesting the hay and bringing it in for the winter. The boys and my uncle went about the field with the family's tractor and pulled the tall grass from the ground. After it was dried it was piled high onto a type of flatbed that was hitched to the tractor. There was a separate barn down in the field where the hay was driven and stored. All of the bigger children who could handle the pitchforks grabbed forkfuls of hay and piled it up on the barn floor. When the pile became several feet high, the younger children, including myself, were asked to climb up onto the top of the pile and jump all around on it to pat it down. After it was condensed, we were told to stand off to the sides so the boys could throw more forkfuls onto the pile. This was repeated till the barn was as full as they could get it. After we finished we would go into the house and have the most amazing, creamy ice cream. It was cut into slices from the carton and put between these crispy wafers that tasted incredible.

I'm glad I experienced this because it gave me some real insight into how my cousins lived on their farm.

I want to share this next bit that also happened at Glenfarne. Once again it happened when I was quite young.

My younger cousin Nuala, myself, her brother Aiden and my brother Tom were left at the house one night while the grownups went to a wedding reception. It was just assumed back then that we would be okay by ourselves for a few hours while they were out and we were, for the most part.

Now, there was no electricity at the thatched-roof house during this time so it was quite dark at night. There had been a light rain earlier in the evening so the ground was wet and the leaves on the trees seemed to be weighted down more so than a day filled with bright sunlight.

As nightfall came there was thunder in the distance. There was a small fire burning in the fireplace so that gave us some light in the main room of the house. The atmosphere quieted down outside and the rain changed to a light drizzle. I was starting to doze a little when a single clamor of thunder exploded right over the top of the house. Nuala screamed and started to cry and I was shaking so badly from it that my brother and Aiden held on to us to make us stop. Nuala would not stop crying and I couldn't blame her. The thunder was so loud the house shook under our feet. And the floor being made only of a thin layer of stone, we thought it would crumble beneath us. Tom was rummaging through the drawers in the cabinets. He told me later that he was looking for a flashlight. Nuala didn't know if her father had one but told him that he did have a lantern and used it at times like this, but the lantern was out with the cow as that was where he had used it last. Rain was coming down through the chimney and splashing onto the fire. It dimmed it somewhat but did not put it out. There were more flashes of lightning along with another crash of thunder and of course this was followed by more screaming and crying from my younger cousin.

After finding no matches, candles or any other type of portable light, my brother decided that the best thing to do was to get under the covers on one of the beds and stay there. He grabbed my sweater at the elbow and started nudging me towards the back of the house which served as the temporary guest room. But then he stopped cold. He shouted for Aiden and told Nuala and me to head into the back room. I overheard him say in a panicked voice that he swore he saw somebody coming up the long driveway headed towards the house. I watched them from the back room crouched by the table waiting for the lightning to prove him right. I think that was the only time I ever heard my brother scream. He was nine years old then and had every right to be scared. Sure enough there was indeed a figure coming up the long driveway. He lost sight of him in one of the curves of the road but as the road straightened, the figure reappeared staggering towards the house. More lightning led to more thunder and more carrying on not only by Nuala but I had joined her in her symphony of tears. I didn't know what to do then so being the eldest girl at the ripe old age of seven, I took hold of Nuala and tried to wrap my small arms around her as much as I could reach. I got her to sit down on the floor with me under the window. I folded her face into my upper body in order to block the bright flashes in the night sky. I looked up only once to see if the sky was still angry and as I did a face shot through the window making direct eye contact with me. The calming did Nuala no good because I screamed so loudly at seeing the face that I made her cry out again. I tried to press us both into the wall so that we could disappear into it. There was a severe pounding on the wooden slat door and a man's voice demanding to be let in. Aiden shouted that it was Uncle Peter and that we'd better let him in. Tom opened the door and in swayed Nuala's dad.

"Why aren't ye all 'en bed yet?" Was all he said.

He took his overcoat off, threw it onto the chair by the fire, grumbled something undecipherable and stammered off to bed.
He had merely tied a few drinks on and decided to walk home from the reception.

After his arrival home and after standing around staring at each other, we went to bed for the night.

Sometime later, after the rain, these long slug-like insects were inching their way up the wall. I saw a few of them here and there but they never bothered us. It was a cottage in the middle of the countryside so there were bugs here and there. That was normal.

The following morning, my cousin Nuala and I were playing in the far creek bed when I mentioned to her that I thought I heard a 'baaa' sound. She looked at me and laughed and imitated the sound. I thought it was her making the sound but a few seconds later we both heard it and she laughed again. Out of nowhere came this lone sheep flying over the wooden fence. It ran by us and kept going. She laughed so hard and made me laugh too. The nearest farm was a quarter mile away so nobody knew where this sheep had come from. But, nonetheless, we told the boys about it and they didn't believe us! The sheep showed up again later and the boys tried to catch it. It nipped at one of their hands and got away from them.

The mud at the cottage was insane at times. In places like Western New York when it rains people say things like, *"My backyard is a sponge!"* or *"My grass looks like a swamp!"* In Glenfarne the mud could be as deep as your knees and you could often lose your wellingtons trying to cross it. It made a terrible sucking noise as it tried to steal away your boots!

When heading out to collect the turf for the stove or fire, the "wellies" would always be worn to keep our shoes from getting covered with the heavy muck.

It was quite difficult for children to pull their own feet out of the mud. Parents got mad when boots were left behind because their child could not retrieve his boots from it. Yuck!

Gathering the turf in Co. Leitrim.

There were always sing-alongs when the family got together. The sheet music and booklets were brought out and we all sang traditional Irish ballads, or any other tunes that most of us knew. This helped keep the magic in the gatherings.

And we all sang the familiar tunes together. It was the tradition.

And we sang some more.

The famous opening words to "Dublin in the Rare Old Times", *"Raised on Song and Stories....."*, composed by Pete St. John, tells of how many of the Irish grew up. Songs and stories were given to new generations at family gatherings and everybody had one to share.

These were precious times and I always kept the stories a part of my own life. I constantly pestered my aunts and uncles to tell and retell specific events that were entertaining in some aspect. My Aunt Margaret told me one day to write them all down and keep a notebook. I am sure glad that I took her advice because I have forty seven spiral-bound tablets full of stories. This book you are reading now is the start of my journey of sharing what I have collected over the years.

Mom and me, our last flight together to Ireland.

**Mike, our pilot, from our last flight to Ireland.
I merely asked to visit the cockpit
and take his picture. There was no issue
then, in the 1980's.**

I felt as if it was still a time of innocence then. I was allowed to visit the cockpit at a simple request. Our pilot gave me permission to photograph him. I told him, that one day his picture would be in a book all about Ireland. He was a pilot for Aer Lingus at the time, he loved flying to and from his homeland.

DAD'S COUNTY MAYO

My parents came from the west coast of Ireland. Mom was from County Leitrim and dad was from Ballyvary in County Mayo. Ballyvary is a small town near Castlebar in County Mayo. This was dad's hometown. I spent more time with mom's side of the family but I did occasionally visit dad's side from time to time.

Both areas of the country were lush and green. In fact, almost all of Ireland is indeed, lush and green. The hills and mountains were always inviting and sheep and cows can be found grazing in the fields everywhere. There were stone and thatched roofed cottages peeking from groves, the occasional ancient site and rush of sheep crossing the road.

My father's county had just as many beautiful sights as my mother's. Dad's side of the family had more cows than mom's side and I did my best to assist his nieces and nephews one time at bringing the cows in for the evening. I never really knew how difficult this was till I tried it myself. We had several young people scattered about in the field where the cows had been grazing. Everyone had their own job of trying to keep the cows from getting past them. My cousin told me to look 'big' because the taller you looked, the more likely the cows would not get past you so they gave me a spot to stand on a downhill slope. I tried waving my arms in the air. I even bent to grab a long stick on the ground but as I did, one of the cows got past me and someone had to circle around and get her back into the middle of the herd with the rest.

I was the only one who returned to the house covered in mud, clay and a bit of natural fertilizer. Of course this made my mom quite angry and it was not pleasant to be scolded in front of all the cousins when they had on much less muck than me. Sure, they were used to this sort of thing and I was not but it was a fun experience I will admit. My father and I laughed about it later.

This is Hal and Joe. Hal was my father's nickname as a boy. His brother Joe was a bit older than dad. My father always loved animals. Himself and his brother are here holding some tiny kittens.

My memories are a bit choppy from my father's side of the family from the early years. There were so many more cousins and relatives and I did not visit them as often as my mom's side so I do not remember them all and there were so many of them. I seem to recall more of the individual places and animals rather than some of the family members.

I was very young when my mother first brought me to Ireland. What I can recall began from a very young age of about four. I was twenty at my last visit. We had visited during these years of my life every three to four years or so. If there was a special occasion like a wedding we went as well. My mother also wanted me to get to know my grandmother. My father's parents were already passed on when I was adopted and from what I've been told, my father's dad died when he was only ten.

Ballyvary was beautiful. It was full of green hills and winding roads. As in mom's county, many of the roads were quite narrow and I used to tell my friends that the roads reminded me of being on a roller coaster. There were quick twists and turns around bends where you could not see an oncoming vehicle until it was practically touching your bumper. Driving through the countryside on those narrow, tight roads was more than an adventure. If you drove very fast, you took chances with your life.

My father was a trickster. He took pleasure in playing jokes on people. I was told that when he was young he did many off-the-wall things that were either quite bold or down-right dangerous. But that was dad and it was part of his personality then. It made him a fascinating person and it influenced me to take my own chances. He had that flavor about him and it sure made a powerful impression.

One of my father's best buddies back home was a man from County Cavan named Johnny Cahill. He and dad got into all kinds of questionable situations together.

Here is Johnny Cahill sitting on my father's shoulders at O'Brien's Tower on the Cliffs of Moher.

Apparently, standing in front of the tower wasn't enough, they had to climb it as well.

Dad and his buddy Johnny Cahill at The Gap of Dunloe, Co.
Killarney. They were young lads back then.
The original photograph is quite fragile.

Dad and Johnny at "Kate Kearney's Cottage"

My dad's family had a pub that carried the family name. They called it Canning's Bar and Lounge. The house was attached to the pub and you could enter it from a connecting room within the house or from a separate entrance. It had a fire later on and from what I heard there was controversy as to who set it and how the fire began. I was told that the IRA may have been behind it but it didn't make any sense to me that they could be responsible. Another source stated it was an insurance issue but the real truth about the fire still eludes me. The truth now is that as of the writing of this book, the pub was a derelict site. I'm glad I got to visit it while it was quite the hoppin' place. It was where I saw my first Juke Box.

Photos of the Canning Pub when it was still in operation.

My father also started his own Gaelic football team. They were at the top of their game when the team played in Montreal, Canada in 1951. He was the captain of the team and it is said that he was one of the men responsible for bringing Gaelic football the United States.

Dad is in the back row, second from the left.

Though difficult to see here, this is the inscription on the back of the above photo. They called themselves "St. Paul's Irish" and were the senior football champs.

My dad is on the right here. It is the coin toss to begin the game. Note the Irish flag behind them.

Dad, kicking off the ball.

Dad, (on right) and four of his siblings here. Eamon on the left, then Joe and Linda.

My father was one of five. There was himself, brothers Joe and Eamon and sisters, Linda and Maeve. I never met Maeve that I can recall. Uncle Eamon had never been to the United States till my dad became sick, but when he did visit, he was quite a hoot. He came to see my father during the summer of 1994. Our neighbors a few doors down from us had a swimming pool and Eamon took to wearing the smallest, most skimpiest looking *Speedo* style bathing suit that I ever saw on a man in his late 60's.

He walked down to the neighbor's house and sat on their porch to have a wee chat with my neighbor's mother. Her face turned red when she came out the front door to join her daughter on the porch and saw this thin little Irish man looking nearly naked sitting in her favorite chair. When Eamon sat, his slightly aged flabby 'love handles' drooped over the thin waistband of his bathing suit and hid it completely from view. He looked as if he was wearing nothing at all. Her voice squeaked when she tried to introduce herself. After the shocking introductions, I brought Eamon around the back where the pool was and helped him climb the ladder to get in. A few minutes later I spied my neighbor's mother stealing a glimpse through the back window towards the direction of the pool. It was quite amusing.

I had gone to Dublin, Ireland to stay with Aunt Linda in the fall of 1988. There were some very old buildings and sites I wanted to explore in and around Dublin and I was grateful that she allowed me and my cousin to stay with her. She had a house near a pier where the *Sea-Link* docked as well as other boats and much larger ships. It was fascinating to watch the boats arrive in the harbor, especially as the sun was setting.

Like Uncle Eamon, Aunt Linda was also an interesting character. It was at this time in my life that I learned what a 'nite-cap' was. She kept offering me a wee nip o'this or a wee nip o'that but I never knew what was in that dark colored bottle so I graciously declined. And there was another interesting tidbit about Aunt Linda and how she used or rather re-used those dark colored bottles. Many of the Irish, during my childhood, would leave a hot water bottle for you placed under the covers of the bed so when you folded back the bed sheets a nice warm and toasty bottle was there warming the bed. Aunt Linda mastered the technique of using some of her best booze bottles as bed warmers by wrapping them in a sock with a knot tied at the top so the bottle wouldn't slip out and burn your skin. It worked quite well and served the purpose. I'd like to assume that she was never concerned about running out of bottles.

I met Uncle Joe only once when I was very little. He liked to sing and tell stories and the looks of bewilderment he got from the rest of the family as he told his stories made me wonder where the stories came from. I know that he also had an appreciation of animals and had a few pets in his lifetime.

My brother Tom and dad took a trip to Ireland together in the 1980's. They visited the Aran Islands and saw the old forts and sites. My father wanted Tom to see the Canning grave site as well. So as a part of their adventure together this was included in the trip and my brother got see the grave of the man he was named after.

Tom in the Aran Islands.

On the Aran Islands.

My brother Tom at the Canning family plot.

Dad lived very close to the Cliffs of Moher. They were his backyard.

Even though my father is gone now, I can still hear his voice in my head belting out the lyrics to *"The Wabash Cannonball"* and *"Shenandoah"*. He was fond of singing and was always turning tunes around, some with his own words and then he would laugh out loud again and again.

THE KEAVENYS AND MCTERNANS
"ONE OF A KINDS"

The Keavenys and McTernans were very good friends of my parents. They were two married couples who lived in Canada. These two couples were some of my favorite family friends growing up. The McTernans owned a house in Cobourg, Ontario and the Keavenys had a home not too far from Toronto on a street appropriately named Athlone Road.

Anne and Charlie McTernan. Uncle Peter, Aunt Dolly and mom.

Peter Keaveny's brother had a farm up the road from my grandmother's thatched cottage in Leitrim, Ireland. I visited it once and remember three very large, hairy sheep dogs. There were sheep on the farm and the owner of the land was very welcoming. I was so young then and I don't remember the conversations spoken, but the sheep dogs he had were beautiful. I was told there was one more roaming about but he was out exploring the field at that particular moment. I remember how fond he was of the dogs and how well trained they were.

I loved to visit Keaveny's house in Ontario. It was cozy, comfortable and fun. Their son Kevin had a huge appreciation for music and I would love it when he played the records in their beautifully finished basement. I asked him to play the same record every time I visited. It was *"Breakfast in America"* by the group Supertramp. There was a comfortable padded desk chair in front of the stereo and I would sit in it and spin around and around till someone asked me to stop. I never got dizzy from all that spinning. It was physically stimulating to go 'round and 'round while the tunes were playing out loud.

The basement in Keaveny's house was a world all its own. Peter and Dolly hosted a dance down there one time when the grownups were in their younger years. It was awesome to watch the adults waltz to the Irish tunes and sing along with the others. They were remembering their own enchanting times as they shared dances with one another. It was a blessing to be there and witness that moment. It was magical and inspiring and I began to see and understand the sacred bond of the friendships as it created a permanent happy memory for me.

Dolly and Peter had a dog named "Laddie" and he was one of my best friends of all time. He was a type of sheep dog mix and was so adorable. His floppy ears were hidden in the fur on his head. He was the only dog who befriended my dog too. Tara and Laddie were best buddies.

Tara and Laddie putting their best paws forward.

Laddie knew how to play the piano, or so I was told when we visited once. A framed picture stood on a corner shelf in the Keaveny's dining room of the talented dog sitting on the piano bench with his paws on the keys. He was looking straight ahead in deep concentration contemplating his next score. I loved this dog. He is the dog I give credit to for making me fall in love with all pooches.

When I was in second grade, my parents surprised my brother and myself with a puppy of our own and since then, my heart was over the moon. I believe that Laddie may have been responsible for this.

Laddie, showing one of his many talents.

Peter Keaveny was an incredible individual. He was one of the most talented people I ever knew and I am grateful to have known him and be influenced by him. He created and built so many different apparatuses during his lifetime. He remodeled his own basement several times and even added a gorgeous full cedar closet. I would open the door of it on several occasions to just to get a whiff of that cedar. He installed a walk in shower in his basement, a beautiful bedroom and a cozy sitting room in the back. He even 'installed' bars on the windows to keep out any unwanted visitors by making it look like they were real. On the outside of the house, it looked like real steal bars, but on the inside, the bars could be easily removed in case there was ever a need to.

The man was a genius and he loved to show my dad his latest and greatest inventions each time we visited. Uncle Peter was a very hip individual when it came to modern technologies and had his very own 'Skype' long before the rest of the population. He brought me to the the the Toronto Science Museum on a few different occasions and he encouraged me to explore, seek and learn about all the different hands on displays. I credit Uncle Peter with my interest in Science and Archaeology.

His wife, Dolly or Nora as was her proper name, was an amazing sort as well. She was a caring mother and one my mom's best friends. She was like a second mother to me and influenced me a great deal too. She took very good care of us all when we visited and took a special interest in my own personal health. On one particular visit, I had been suffering from terrible anxiety due to final exams and testing at school. She had me sit in front of her on the floor while her magical hands rubbed my shoulders and back. Within a short while every tight notch of tension I had brought with me was gone. She managed to relieve me of all my stress. She was an amazing lady.

Everybody was provided for when we visited them and the meals we ate while we visited were perfect. She supported her husband Peter with all his little and not so little projects and the two of them taught me how a marriage worked. They fused their lives together and helped each other with almost everything and the end results were always successful. What a great model to follow.

Dolly, Peter and Laddie here in front of their house on Athlone Rd.

The McTernans owned a house in Cobourg, Ontario. In was near Cobourg Beach and Lake Ontario. Anne had told me once that they loved their house but could really only enjoy its location for three months out of the year, later on I understood why. The house was close to the lake and I believed that the winters were probably quite cold.

I loved visiting Cobourg. I was grateful as a child that my parents were friends with them. We were invited to stay at their house several times and could visit the beach as often as we wanted throughout our stay with them.

Charlie had an enormous garden in his back yard and grew all kinds of veggies and plants. They had a shed to one side and in it were two rubber inner tubes that my brother and I were allowed to use at the beach. I always asked about the tubes when we visited hoping that each time they would be inflated waiting for me. I loved beach toys.

What a great atmosphere Cobourg had. One day, when I was about six or seven, Anne gave me an entire loaf of bread that I was allowed to take to the beach and feed the seagulls. Times were different then and children were allowed to feed the gulls. What was special about that particular day was that I got hundreds of seagulls to follow me back to their house. I dropped small pieces of bread, a little at a time and got all the birds to stay with me all the way back to the house. Someone took a picture and some of the neighbors remembered this but I never got to see the photograph.

We used to bring our dog Tara to Cobourg and to Keaveny's too. I was on the beach one time with her and I was digging a hole in the sand when the dog began digging also. A reporter from a local newspaper came by and asked if I could get the dog to do it again. I began digging a hole and sure enough, Tara copied me. The woman laughed and got her picture.

There is a really neat pier and lighthouse at Cobourg. The pier is old but folks are still allowed to walk out onto it. If you are careful, you can make your way all the way to the lighthouse and touch it. I finally did so later on and my Uncle Peter took a video for me. I had always wanted to touch the famous lighthouse. I finally did and my uncle videotaped it.

The Lighthouse at Cobourg Beach, Ontario. One of the best spots in the world for sunsets.

MY COMICAL, YET STEADFAST IRISH PARENTS

Quirks of an Irish Mom

My mom was very funny at times. You could laugh with her and at her. She had a thick Irish brogue that my friends loved to imitate. They would twist the sides of their mouths up to get the words right and crack up every time. The quirky things my mom would do and some of the superstitions she believed were funny enough on their own, but when you added an Irish accent and tried to explain what everything meant, the situations were even funnier.

My teachers at school were concerned when it was time for parent-teacher conference nights because nobody could understand mom due to her thick Irish accent. I told my teachers that all they had to do was smile and keep nodding their heads and everything would be fine.

My mother was the original multi-tasker. She could sit at the kitchen table, shake her leg and sip her tea while staring you down pointing a finger of accusation all at the same time. She was always blaming somebody for something, even if she was the culprit. She would never admit that she was wrong about anything.

Mom's emotions were elusive. I knew her, yet never knew her. A bruised knee or scraped elbow brought shouts of upset so lessons were learned early enough not to seek her sympathy regarding boo-boos. She was a tough cookie in that respect. She wasn't a touchy-feely type of mom but my love for her was boundless.

At times she was cat-like. She could sneak up quietly and pounce when candy was eaten before dinner and the stern, dungeonous look in her eye told me that I was grounded - again. Her ripe, Irish accent got thicker when she was angry and hearing her curse with that heavy brogue always cracked me up no matter how mad she was. When she got angrier, the accent got thicker and I would imitate her. Then we both burst into laughter. It was at those moments that I loved her the most. Her laughter was priceless. It was real and not forced and sometimes she laughed so hard it left us both teary eyed.

She towered over most moms at a height of six-foot-two. Yet even though she was a willful pillar of strength, there was an innocence about her. She hid something. Perhaps it was a vulnerability from childhood. There was a softness and a powerful feminine side to mom. Somewhere, deep behind her emerald eyes, there was a side to her rarely seen, but I knew it was there. It had to be, because she'd laugh when I tried to copy her bold accent and quirky Irish ways.

Her booming voice was a shield. It could be heard clanging on every level of the house and three doors away in the summertime. But besides her powerful voice and taller than average height, mom was also known for her Irish soda-bread. The iron kettle that baked it was forged in Ireland. It was worn and handle-less but yielded endless perfect loaves. Mom's magical way of kneading and turning the dough round and round into the best tasting soda bread was the talk of her Irish circle. She had long abandoned the native, Gaelic recipe, but mastered its creation. I often heard her singing away in the kitchen, the rhyming lines of *"It's a Long Way to Tipperary"* or *"Four Green Fields"* as she sculpted out the raisin-filled treat.

A week or two before St. Patrick's Day we'd receive many phone calls. Friends and family were clamoring to be the lucky ones, chosen by Frances, to present her famous loaf to honored guests at their celebratory feasts. She did her best to accommodate everybody so no one was ever turned away. She accommodated everybody as that was her way.

My mother had a strong affection for animals, including wild critters of the woods. Back home in Manorhamilton, she often left scraps and other tidbits behind the house. She never turned away any creature in need of a meal. What she had, she shared and if she didn't have it to share she went to get it so that all were satisfied.

She also had several dogs as a child so when my brother and I begged for a puppy, there was only one day of deliberating. Our little tan pup came to us by way of the Buffalo Irish Club in South Buffalo. The wee thing was in need of a home and we were in need of a dog, so the fates brought us together. The family that gave her to us brought her to the Irish Center and just like the old *"Irishman's Shanty"* tune, tied her to the leg of the table until it was time to go home. Mom felt it was her place to name the dog and chose a renowned area from back home. The dog was appropriately named Tara. Tara lived seventeen long years and was an amazing best friend.

A Motorcycle mom?

"Sister Josie" and her cup 'tea at the kitchen table. All the members of her respiratory class, wanted to dress up and play a joke on their instructor, so mom was "Nun for a Day."

Mom got to name our dog.
Tara with dad and my brother Tom.

Tara.

Here is a funny story that concerned my mom and her quirky way of thinking.

A wicker decoration hung on our living room wall for nearly four years. It was a hat because it had a brim and a band that circled around it. A strap hung down that was secured on both sides. Several clusters of plastic flowers hung from its trim. It was pretty and spring-like, but there was a problem. If you gently brushed against it, flowers fell out of it so picking up its fallen branches became a regular occurrence, but mom liked the hat so there it stayed.

One afternoon, I was sitting in the living room contemplating my thoughts, when the hat casually dropped an unusual amount of flowers but this time nobody was near it. I stared at the wicker ornament in wonder and suddenly realized that mom's hat was not a hat at all but a basket. She had nailed it to the wall upside down. That brim that she thought was the rim of the hat was trim of the basket and the strap that hung down was the basket's handle. I called her to come take a look at it. She stammered into the living room wondering what all the nonsense and fuss was about. I told her my theory, but she insisted the item was a hat. She snatched up the fallen branches, briskly shoved them into the straw, turned and marched out of the room.

Several weeks later I was in my bedroom when one of her Irish cronies came to visit. After a short conversation in the kitchen, mom led her friend into the living room. I stuck my head out to listen because they were talking about the hat! I tip-toed towards the conversation and peeked around the corner. Mom was pointing towards the object in question. Her friend asked the moment she saw it.

"Josie, why do 'ye have a basket hangin' upside down on the wall?"

"Hannah, that's not a basket. I know it's a hat, how can it be a basket? It's a hat! That's the strap hangin' down there." She was quite annoyed with the decoration and with me for questioning her about it to begin with. Her friend stood scratching her head.

"Josie, look, if you flip it over, the flowers won't fall out of it. And that strap hangin' down, 'tis not a strap, 'tis the basket's handle."

"Jaysus! Why would I hang a basket upside down on the wall? It's a hat, I'm tellin' ye' and do ye' think I'm stu-putt?"

Moments like that kept me laughing through the years. Even her friends found her situations quite entertaining. The neighbors loved to talk to me, imitating her accent as well as her odd mannerisms. Yes, mom and her quirky Irish ways were the talk of the neighborhood. She kept everybody on their toes, but they kept an eye on her too because there was always a story to tell from just about anything she did.

I had a projector screen standing up in the basement so I could show her and some neighbors a film I made in class at school. When the movie started she shouted out loud that the paneling on the wall behind the screen was crooked. The movie screen was tilted and needed to be straightened up but she insisted it was the paneling. This story too, was repeated many times over the years whenever we wanted to get mom riled up again and she would laugh at it and herself and so would we.

My father brought me home a cute little Irish stuffed bear from one of his trips back home. One day when I came home from school, I found that the bear was not in his usual place centered on my bed near my pillow. I then heard my dad chuckling around the corner. It was always one of those 'I wonder how long it will take her to notice' games he was playing. He made me search for the bear till I found it. It was always in some strange place too, on top of the fridge, in the oven, the bathtub, behind the sofa, in the fridge, in a cupboard, in the dog's bed and even in the mailbox! He was a trickster and he loved to play his little jokes on me constantly.

He died when I was twenty-five and I thought my life was over. We had a great friendship together and I couldn't face him leaving me but he was suffering from Non-Hodgkin's Lymphoma and it took him. His pain had finally ended.

My brother Tom entered the US Air Force in the late 1980's and dad was devastated that his only son was leaving home. Once Tom had moved out I decided it was my place to become dad's best friend. I felt sorry for him and he seemed so depressed because his best buddy and only son was headed for Basic Training. I took it upon myself to pretend to like football, hockey and WWII.

It was then I began asking my dad about the war he was in and how he dealt with it. He had quite a few stories to tell and one of my favorites is included here. It's a quirky one about an owl, the snow and his life.

Christmas Eve, 1943

Owls are sacred to the many of the Irish. And Christmas Eve is an old time for miracles. Maybe one of them happened in my family, on the darkest of nights at the darkest of times when the world was at war.

Harry Canning was hired by a mail delivery service in England in 1943. One of his duties was to assist the British Red Cross by distributing medical kits, letters and food packages to POW's in Germany. My dad was fiercely instructed to carry identification, wear a special uniform and patch at all times. This designated his position to anyone he came in contact with. The ten thousand medical packages sent from the Red Cross in United States in 1943, were not enough to cover the demand for the American POW's so Britain did what they could to assist the allied prisoners.

My father could not serve in the Army due to a childhood injury, but he was pleased to have a duty where he could deliver the needed kits and letters from home.

He often said that winter in Germany at that time, was biting cold and told me that the air was often filled with a slight smell of powdery, artillery after-blast. It would waft through the night sky, reach his frozen nostrils and force him to cover his face with his gloves.

He said he had to create a mind set for himself as he delivered the packages. He focused so much on his duty to keep him from remembering the wounds and ailing situations of the men.

Whenever he had a chance, or wherever he was invited, he would always share a happy story or tell a joke as he went about delivering the parcels. Sometimes, soldiers or guards invited him into their huts, sharing chocolates and telling stories of their own.

On Christmas eve in 1943, there was a larger amount of mail and parcels than usual. After his last delivery, he headed into the brisk night in the direction of a social gathering. It was at a local pub of sorts, where he was invited to celebrate the holiday. The wind pierced his skin and sent snowflakes billowing into his face like tacks.

As he walked along in the night chill, he thought about another gathering taking place that same evening. He paused on the road a moment to shield his face from the cold and caught sight of a small white owl perched atop a wooden post facing his direction. The owl stirred as he walked towards it, stretched its wings and changed the direction it was facing. It seemed to somehow communicate to him and tell him to turn around. My father thought it odd that the owl did not fly off as he approached it. After pondering about the odd bird, he turned and went in a different direction. He decided to attend the holiday vigil rather than the row at the pub. The cold air seemed to lessen as he headed in the direction of the vigil and the wind subsided to stillness. He turned to catch a final glimpse of his friend on the post but it was no longer there. Perhaps it too, had its own gathering to attend.

There was a small make-shift Christmas tree in the back of the assemblage room. He noted that crude ornaments had been made from silver paper, similar to the kind found in packets of cigarettes. Whatever was available was what was on the tree. It was enough to give the room an ambiance of Christmas. He remembered to pray for everyone involved in the war. He was grateful for his place in it all but wished it was over. He enticed some of the attendees to play a quick game of his Gaelic football after the service. They gladly obliged.

When the vigil concluded, my father received word that the assemblage he initially set out to attend had a worse fate. An explosion of artillery leveled the pub that same evening and there were no survivors.

Was it the white owl that made him change his mind? I am ever so grateful for that owl and for my father's decision to attend the vigil that evening.

In a different setting, time and place another story that was told to me about dad was how his buddies got him quite tipsy one particular evening and dressed him up in women's clothing. Then they got him up on a stage where he sang his heart out. He told me that he never, ever did such a thing but knowing his trickster and goofy nature, I have a feeling that he did.

My dad loved fishing and shared this passion with my brother and myself. Mom was not as thrilled as we were because she was the one who had to scale the fish and prepare them for the grill.

Mom on the left and a friend with tonight's dinner.

My dad taught me how to fish and I loved it a great deal. I enjoyed fishing off the dock at Tom Johnson's cottage on Rushford Lake in New York. It was a great place to fish even though the lake was manmade.

Tom Johnson's dock at Rushford Lake.

"Dinner!"

"And Breakfast!"

Dad knew how to work those single-crank motor boats that were around in the 1970's. He knew the waterways and was educated on how to steer a boat and sail it through all kinds of waves and such. I am grateful to him for knowing what he knew because he was able to rescue two of his boating buddies on the Niagara River in the 1980's when the boat he was in crashed into the breakwall.

My dad, a neighbor and her friend had gone fishing before sunup on a Saturday morning in the summer of the early 1980's. They had taken a Styrofoam cooler with drinks and food since they had planned to be out all day and evening. Our neighbor's friend had got himself a new boat and was waiting to try it out on the Niagara River so off they went.

They didn't catch much throughout the day so when evening came, the owner of the boat wanted to continue fishing till he was satisfied with catching something worthwhile. He wanted to head out further into Lake Erie, leaving the Niagara River. As it became dark, my dad suggested they start heading back because mist and fog began to make it very difficult to see. The boat owner kept pleading to keep fishing as my dad kept saying how he was losing sight of anything familiar around them. After a few moments of looking around all sides of the boat he thought he saw a distant, single bluish light coming from what must have been the shore.

So then, as the fog got thicker, it was decided that they better hurry back and get in. The motor was revved up and they started racing towards the direction of the blue light, where they believed the shoreline to be, or so they thought. Just a few moments after they sped up, they crashed hard into something and all three passengers were thrown from the boat. My dad was a stocky fellow then so he merely tipped over backwards into the water. My neighbor was quite thin and a lightweight individual. She was thrown quite a distance from the boat and her friend was as well.

When my dad resurfaced, he called out the two names of his companions and heard the female voice first. He tried to get his bearings in the water and looked up and around to see if he could see anything. What he did see was a round, glowing blue 'ball' that was held by a woman wearing a long, straight dress standing on the rocks not too far from where he was. He then found my neighbor clinging to a rock in the water and helped her towards the blue light. He then found her friend hanging onto the opposite side of the damaged boat and helped him to the rocks as well. They all climbed onto the rocks and stayed there till daylight.

When they were able to see around them, there was no sign of the blue light anywhere. My dad asked the other two if they had seen the female on the rocks but they did not. They couldn't believe their eyes at where they found themselves either. They hadn't a clue where they had crashed the boat. They were almost back where they had launched the boat and were so close to the shore and didn't know it. The fog had been so thick and they were very far into the lake and were dumbfounded as to what had happened. The boat was beyond repair but it didn't sink. It was partially caught up in the rocks on the breakwall of the Niagara River.

Later on my father told me that once they hit something, all he wanted to do was call me on the new, push button purple phone he had just installed in my bedroom for me the night before. He said he was thinking of me and I know that I must have felt it, because when it was four o'clock in the morning and they were not back yet, I began to worry. I had told my mom I felt something was wrong and I kept trying to convince her of it. They were able to get help and came home shaken but all in one piece. My dad told me about the woman he believes he saw on the bank.

Every year, on the anniversary of the accident that he survived, I drop roses into the Niagara River to thank the lady for showing him where the land was.

My father and two of his best buddies started the Buffalo Irish Club or Center in South Buffalo in 1970. I was told they leased the building until they had enough money to purchase it.

It was here I learned how to swim. My dad encouraged me to swim into the deeper end of the pool and in no time at all it was as if I had been in the water all my life.

I am ever so grateful to him for teaching me how to swim because I was able to rescue a drowning boy when I was four years old. We had been staying at a cottage in Picton in Canada when a little toddler wandered into the lake, lost his footing and went under the water. I swam to where he fell and was able to get him above water and back to the shore. I was scolded for going into the water, but then the grownup saw the reason why and understood.

I wandered off when I was small one time at Picton and everybody was sent out to look for me. One of the older children found me curled up in the belly of a cow at the farm of the man who owned the cottages. I loved his cow and she was the first animal that allowed me to feed her by hand so I wanted to visit with her again later that day. What's wrong with that?

Me and Betsy, my cow friend.

Years later just before the snowy and icy "Blizzard of '77", Tom Johnson, my dad's friend who owned the cottage at Rushford Lake, invited us to visit the cottage in the winter. He wanted my father to see the manmade lake and how it was drained back. Rumor has it that there was a small city under the lake and possibly a very large tree. The lake in fact did look very odd when the water was drained back.

Tom Johnson also invited his brother and their son John as well. Paul Johnson, Tom's youngest son, knew of a great place to go sledding and told me and my brother to bring our sleds, so we did.

Paul Johnson, me, John Johnson and Tom

On one of the afternoons, my brother Tom, Paul Johnson, John Johnson and me headed out with my red plastic sled. Behind the cottage there was a road and a short way down on the other side of the road there was a two-by-four wooden slab across a creek bed. We crossed the creek and walked through woods. I wanted to get ahead of the boys so I ran the rest of the way through the open field and eventually came to the base of a tall hill. It was a strange hill. I began to climb the side of it. There seemed to be extra wide steps that were a part of the hillside. They went all the way to the top where the hill flattened out. I couldn't wait to get across the top of the hill and sled down the other side. I looked down the hill and saw the boys heading through the field. I started to cross the flat top of the hill when I began to sink down into the snow. It was getting deeper but my excitement of getting to the other side kept me going. I heard a loud crack.

All at once icy cold water began to fill my boots. I took a few a more steps forward and the water began to fill the mandatory snowsuit that my mom made me wear. It began to get quite heavy. I jumped forward into the water on my stomach as I learned to do when I was swimming at the Buffalo Irish Club. I thought I could swim to the other side of the water. When I got to the middle I went completely under the ice. I kept trying to get to the other side. When I got there, I tried to climb out but my snowsuit was so wet that it compacted the snow underneath me and made the slope of the bank hard and frozen. The more I tried climbing out, the more I slid back down into the water.

After several tries I put my head on my arm and tried to cry but my face began to freeze. It was at that moment that I just gave up.

Now, I don't know if I fell asleep or not but a short while later, I heard a sound in the distance. I heard something like a large group of houses galloping or loud thunder far off away from the hill. The sound got closer and louder and when I lifted my head to see what I could, I saw a small group of children taking large leaps through the snow headed in my direction. They were laughing as if they were playing a game. It was almost as if the galloping sound and their laughter were one in the same.

One of the children jumped into the water behind me and two more either side of me. The two on the sides each grabbed an arm and the one behind me grabbed a clump of material from the snowsuit near my lower back. They flew me up and out of the water and left me down in the snow. And that was how the boys found me. They got me onto the sled and pulled it all the way back down the hill, through the field and forest and back to the cottage.

My father kept asking Tom what happened after I told him I was in the water, but all my brother said was that I was already out of the water when they found me. I kept telling my dad and Tom Johnson that the little boys and girls got me out of the water but they didn't know what I was talking about.

My dad got me out of the snowsuit and they were shocked that it stood up all its own against the wall. That is how frozen it was. I kept repeating to everybody that little boys and girls had gotten me out of the water and my brother concurred again that I was already out of the pond and several feet away from the pond's bank when they found me.

Tom Johnson knew of the area near that hill but phoned the owner who had a cottage nearest to it. He was told that the pond was manmade and was used as a dew pond so his corn field below would not get flooded in the spring when the rain and thaw came down the side of the hill. The neighbor also told him that the pond was several feet deep and couldn't believe that I was able to crawl out of it but was glad I did.

And the more I repeated the story about the boys and girls getting me out, the more strange and odd looks I got from my family.

To this day. I am grateful to whomever got me out of that frozen pond. I will never forget the sound of the cracking ice underneath me as I tried moving through the water. I have lost some of my hearing in my left ear due to going under the water but that was the only affect I suffered. Again, I am ever so grateful to the little boys and girls who got me out!

I loved my father's sense of humor. I didn't really notice it till he and I became good friends later on, but I'm glad it was there. He kept me laughing during the times we did have together.

I am on the roof, helping him clean the gutters when he decides to sic the dog on me.

I told him that his feet would make a great
design on a greeting card. He laughed when
he saw this picture. (Yes, those really are his feet!)

Dad made many people laugh. He bartended
for the Buffalo Irish Club for several years.

Irish Swearin'

One of the famous Irish expletive sayings when they are frustrated is,
"*Jay-sus, Mary and Joseph!*" Now, my parents names were Harry and Josie.
So when I wanted to make fun of the popular phrase as well as mom and
dad, I would often shout out, "*Jay-sus, Harry and Josie!*" Mom, of course,
would scream back at me in her thick, Irish accent.

"*Eileen, dammit, stop swearin'!*" It wouldn't be complete if she didn't add
"dammit" to her cursing me out for swearing.

We always ended up laughing afterwards. No matter what was said.

My father wanted a fun and wacky picture he could send to his niece in Ireland so he asked me to come up with something off-the-wall. It was a few weeks away from St. Patrick's Day and we had snow on the ground, so I got myself a can of green spray paint and made a large image of a three leaf clover in the snow for him. After the picture was developed, he laughed out loud and told his niece that he had something interesting coming to her in the mail. I took a second picture of the shamrock to keep for myself and all of his other family members wanted their own copy of it as well.

My parents both helped organize a sendoff party for John and Evelyn Sullivan at the Buffalo Irish Club. They decided to move to California, to be with some of their kids and be in a warmer climate.

A few of the fun-loving men at the center dressed up as the happy couple and performed a skit in their honor. Sadly, not long after they moved John's life came to an end when a car hit him while he was riding his bike, something he did for years in Buffalo without a single incident.

My mom can be seen on the far right, laughing like crazy at the two pretending to be John and Evelyn. Mom missed her friend very much but kept in touch.

INTERESTING PLACES IN IRELAND

In 1988 I was finally able to visit some places that I had dreamed of going to in Ireland. I am fascinated with the older cultures of Ireland as well as the folklore and stories that have been handed down over the ages.

One of the places I visited is in Dublin. It is called St. Michan's Church and it was built around 1095. The church itself is beautiful and still has the organ and pipes that George Frederick Handel used to rehearse his "Messiah". But if you get to visit this particular location, you must go around to the back of the church to metal door. There is a sanctuary under the church where real mummies have been discovered. When I visited there in 1988, photos were not allowed due to the sensitivity of the atmosphere down there but a family member of mine gave me a picture that he took himself without a flash camera. I have been told that the image here is three nuns. I also heard it was different people altogether. It is believed that at one time a very old forest covered most of Dublin and when the trees were cleared to build the city, the roots were left deep in the ground and created the natural tannic acid. This is something I learned that the Egyptians used in the past for natural mummification.

My Aunt Margaret once told me that the word Dublin actually means "Black Pool". She was one of the first people to tell me that there is a whole other city under the streets of Dublin. I know that the catacombs do go quite a distance themselves. There are some famous folks down there who were a part of an Irish rebellion as well as several others. Be careful where you step!

Below the sanctuary of the church are the older graves of many Irish citizens.

These fine folks of Ireland are well preserved down below in the catacombs of the church. The fellow in the back, is deemed a giant and nicknamed, "The Crusader." It was good luck to rub his pinky finger at the time.

The fella they nicknamed "The Crusader".
Might be due to the way his legs were crossed over himself.
I was told he is several feet tall.

Since 2007, I have been giving presentations on Irish and Celtic Folklore all over Western New York and in Dufferin, Ontario in Canada. The community or continuing education programs have hosted my talks in West Seneca, Hamburg, Elmira, Lackawanna and the Roycroft Campus in East Aurora. I have also presented at The Niagara Celtic Festival in Olcott, New York. I felt it was appropriate to kick these off at a very special location. I chose the Buffalo Irish Club for my initial workshop. I share slides and stories of where I've been, what I've seen and what I've heard and collected. I created different programs all with the Celtic or Irish overhead.

"Haunted Ireland: Exploring Beyond the Castle Walls" has been quite popular everywhere I have given it. "Lore of the Celtic Goddess" is interesting as well and "Ancient, Sacred Ireland" is one of my favorites. "A Bit 'O the Irish Lore" is a humorous one. I enjoy performing them all. I have learned so much about history and the stories of Ireland and I know that there is so much more to know and learn.

As I mentioned earlier, I am grateful to my aunt for suggesting that I write down the stories I was told. It is several of these stories as well as many more that I share at my presentations.

As I became an adult, the fascination of the ancient castles and old abbeys stayed with me and I wanted to explore more places and talk to more people. I wanted to hear first hand, what people had to say about what they were told as children. There are a quite a few interesting tales there as well.

Teamhair or Tara is one part of Ireland, I just had to visit. My father's surname "Canning" can be traced all the way back to King O'Cannanain who was a High King that ruled for a time at Tara. Many of Tara's kings just might be buried at Tara as well. Parts of the ground there are quite bumpy and uneven as you walk through the site. There are two excavated graves there as well. I was told by a visitor there that they might be the tombs of Tia Tephi's sons who came to Ireland when Moses was fleeing Egypt.

I keep an open mind whenever I get stories from people because history is so full of lore and legend that nobody really knows the real histories.

My father was from Co. Mayo and he often told me about Gráinne Ní Mháille, or Grace O'Malley. She was a pirate in Ireland during the time of Queen Elizabeth the First. My dad told me that his father once told him about how Miss Grace is said to haunt Howth Castle and the surrounding area in Dublin. She was refused lodging and was turned away. She kidnapped the son who was the heir to the thrown and took him out to sea with her. Queen Elizabeth made a deal with her that if she returns the son, she would allow her to have lodging at Howth anytime she pleased when she came into Dublin.

A place setting was put down at the table for her and the front gates were left open for her as well. In modern times, when the castle had renovations done, her place setting, that had always been there for her, was removed. Strange and odd things began happening in the castle. Pictures and other decorative items fell from their place on the wall.

It was suggested that her place setting be returned to the table in the main hall. Once it was put back, the unusual events ceased and all was quiet again. From what I've been told, her place setting is still there today and nobody dares to move it.

Knocknarea is a large hill in Co. Sligo. From a distance, it looks like most hills but when you get closer to it you can see a round smaller hill on top of it. The supposed grave of the one and only Queen Medb or Maeve is on top of this hill. There is a very large pile of stones that make up the cairn that she is rumored to be buried under. When I was there, I was told to add a stone to the pile and never take one away because Queen Medb should always remain under that hill. Due to her less than nice ways about herself, she should stay buried forever.

If a person took a stone away with them, the spirit of Medb might follow them home.

**Queen Medb just might be buried
Under this pile of stone on the top of Knocknarea.**

Another interesting place I visited is called, "The Jumping Wall of Kildemock" in County Louth.

**The mysterious "Jumping Wall". Legend
states that this wall jumped over an excommunicated
person that it didn't want buried inside the church. The foundation
and wall are three feet apart.**

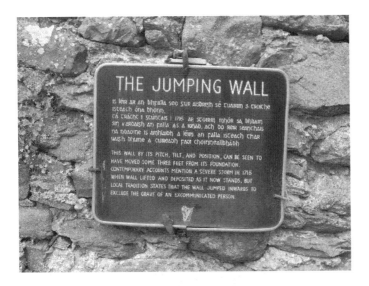

This plaque is mounted on the wall itself, telling of the event and when it took place.

There is a significant difference between the wall and the foundation.

Odd places like this in Ireland have always fascinated me. There is so much history and lore everywhere you visit. The places, stories and people are woven together in an everlasting knot in history.

In my presentations, I keep these places alive and revisit much of the folklore so that those who attend can experience the magic for themselves.

Eileen A. Canning

ODD SOD STORIES
(STRANGE AND UNIQUE STORIES FROM THE OLD SOD HERSELF)

Ireland holds a great deal of history and stories. There have been stories about leprechauns, fairies, ghosts, goddesses and so much more. Many of these tales were written a long time ago and some more recently. I have a few that I added to this book. Some are from my personal experiences and some were told to me by my uncles, aunts or other family members. In fact, on several occasions when we would visit the Old Sod, I would ask my aunts or uncles to tell me the same stories over and over. A great aunt suggested that I write them in a notebook so that I would always have them. I'm glad I listened to her because I have been blessed with many interesting tales of magical or even supernatural events. Now, I don't want to frighten anyone here with the word "supernatural". I simply mean that some of the stories are about subject matter that may be a bit odd or seem strange to a few. I have recorded these stories as they were told to me or as they happened to me personally. I do not wish to change anybody's beliefs with these tales. People experience things in different ways and the following stories are way I remember them.

The first story is called, "The Pillar People." It is something that happened to me when I was very little. It happened to me when I was with a few of the family members driving through the countryside on our way to

Glencar Waterfall. We were away for quite a while and I was dozing on and off in the car. It was something that may have been part dream and part reality but for whatever the reason, this event stayed with me through my childhood and into my adult life. It had a profound enough sensation on me that I wished to include it.

"The Pillar People"

They wanted me to play with them. I saw them coming down the grassy hill. They were steady and light. I jumped from the back seat of the car and ran to them. The grownups were someplace else. I had fallen asleep in the car but woke up and saw the ones I now call The Pillar People. I never saw them before in my life.

There were so many of them. It was like a parade. They cascaded down the gentle hill in such a way that I just had to join them. As I ran amongst them, they bent to acknowledge me. They were fascinating beings and the feeling I got from them was kind and loving.

One of the taller figures came close to me, bent itself at the middle and met me face to face. The visions in its face were incredible. Instead of eyes, I saw two distinct lands. One land was my earthly dimension, the place I knew and the familiar sights of my childhood. The other land was crystallized. Forests and streams, hillsides and groves were shining with crystal accents. I saw moons and suns from other worlds and creatures I did not recognize.

As they floated across the grass barely touching it, the base of their clouded designs meshed with the ground and shook with a subtle vibration. I was happy running and in and around the figures. At one point during my innocent frolic I stood in front of one the opaque beings to see if it wanted to play a game. I did jumping-jacks. It shook itself like a wet dog getting out of bath and it made me laugh.

I asked one of the beings where they were going but didn't receive an answer. I remember the height of my special friends. They were thin and tall "pillars" that seemed to fade in and out from shades of grey to white and back again. I think they were made of fog or mist or even clouds and I think they had feelings too. When I was with them I felt happy and experienced a sense of being free. They emanated the same kind of energy. I was a part of their parade and they didn't seem to mind. I felt as if they already knew me even though I was meeting them for the first time.

It started to rain so I went back to the car. The Pillar People continued down the hill. I watched them fascinated with their sweeping movements. Then something interesting happened, one of the beings stopped moving. As it stood alone, it stretched itself out from top to bottom making itself about twenty feet tall. All of the other "Pillars" went to it and fused with it until it was a single tall, thin individual. It turned into a cloud of white, crystallized mist and floated up several feet to the top of the nearby trees. It hesitated there for a moment, thinned itself even more, turned horizontally and shot off into the light of the day like an arrow.

As I got older, I revisited the memory of these wonderful beings. Sometimes I dreamt about them. I would recall the crystallized land I saw in that misty face. In my dreams I see them living in crystal forests, but sometimes visiting the human realm of Earth.

I am grateful to these beings for enchanting my childhood with a vision so powerful and intriguing. I hope that someday I will run amongst them again. I sincerely believe they are a part of my spirit and I am a part of their crystal land.

The following story took place in County Clare.

My father told me many strange and odd stories that he remembered from his childhood or other family members had shared with him. One that he told me was from County Clare, not too far from his hometown.

There is an old tower on the Cliffs of Moher in County Clare that my dad and his friend climbed when they were young. They were told that a very rich and well-to-do single woman lived in the tower and owned all the land in that area a long time ago. She was so well off that the men of the nearby towns all wanted to marry her so they could share in her riches. She knew this and planned how she would deal with each of them.

My dad was told that she either liked the suitors or she hated them.

Those she liked were invited to spend some time with her above in her tower. She only spent a little time with each of those men and then sent them on their way.

The men she didn't care for she treated quite differently. They were invited up to her tower and given the finest food and drink that she had. She kept these fellows with her late into the evening and kept giving them more and more drink. She made sure it was quite late when they were dismissed. She escorted them down the stairs and back to their horse drawn carriages. As they readied themselves to leave she scurried back up the stairs and raised her lantern to the open narrow window near the top of the tower. By flashing her lantern in this open window, she signaled to the sentry at the bottom of the entryway. This was his signal to turn the guiderails of the cliff toward the sea. The suitors who left her company late at night went down the road away from her tower, off the cliff and into the ocean.

I always thought this story was just a legend, but a family member of mine who worked for a scientific lab at the time had been scoping the sides of the cliff for dinosaur fossils that had been reported when he came across several small bead like pebbles embedded in the rocks. Once soaked in a solvent to dissolve away the debris he discovered that these bead-like objects were a type of ball bearing that had been used in horse drawn carriages from the 1800's. There were hundreds and hundreds more. How many suitors did she send off that dark and foggy cliff?

The White Horse of Glenfarne

When I was in the single digits of my age, my dad bought me my very first camera. I took it everywhere I went. When I visited Ireland, it was one of my most prized possessions that I took with me. It was one of those 110 cameras that had film which needed to be developed after the role was finished.

At my grandmother's farm in Glenfarne there was a little girl visiting from America that was always asking questions. My Uncle Peter must have been reaching the end of his rope in regards to my questioning and told me to take my camera and visit a field that was quite a distance away from the thatched cottage. He said I would know the spot when I found because there were five large stones placed in a small circle there. He told me about a white horse with large, hairy hooves that was often seen in that field. I was at an age to know that he was most likely wanting me to leave him alone so I left with my camera and headed for the little stone circle in the field.

I walked around the circle at through it and then weaved my way in and out of the stones. I looked all around the field and didn't see any white horse with large, hairy hooves.

I sat down in the middle of the stones and looked around some more. There was still no sign of the creature that my uncle told me about. I started to think that it was his ploy just to get me out of the house, stop asking questions and send me to a spot away from the farm. I began to play with the grass and see if I could push one of the stones. Then I stared up at the sky and watched the clouds. I must have dozed off because I awoke with a wet spray of horse nose discharge on my face. I had been sneezed on.

The animal stood above, looking down at me. His head was enormous and I noticed that his ears were two different colors. He was quite friendly and all I wanted to do was wrap my arms around his head and give him a hug. I was a young girl being greeted by a horse on a grassy field in the middle of nowhere. What young girl wouldn't want to have an encounter with a horse that friendly. I thought of my camera after staring at him for a bit and got a photo of his head. I was so excited to see the horse that my uncle mentioned that I almost forgot about my camera.

I had to advance the slide bar on the camera after I took the picture so I flipped it over to do so and when I did and advance it to take another picture the horse turned and trotted off across the field and down the hill. I was so happy about getting a picture of him that I ran like hell back to the house to tell everybody. Nobody was as excited as me. I couldn't believe that nobody was excited about the picture that I took.

Later on my uncle told me, yet again, to take a walk down the long driveway and find a gentleman who lived two farms up the road. He gave me the man's name and told me to ask him about the white horse. He said he would have an interesting story to tell me. I was very excited to be heading out again for another adventure. I found the house and the man and got his story.....

A white horse showed up on a farm one day when the farmer's own plough animal was lame with a sore hoof. It was a tall horse, quite bushy looking as it had an extra thick tail and mane. It had an unusual marking as well. One of its ears was black and the other white and its head almost seemed as if it was too big for its body.

I was told that the animal came at a time when it was needed the most. It showed up in the farmer's front pen one afternoon and allowed the owner of the farm to approach it. He stroked its mane and spoke to it. Apparently he made some kind of offer to the animal and it followed him into the barn. He put his plough equipment onto the horse and led him to a field where the animal knew exactly what to do. The farmer took excellent care of the horse while it was at his farm. It was groomed and given lots of space to move freely about in a large pen.

From what I was told, this particular horse was so friendly and easy going that children were allowed to ride him around on their farmland. He was a godsend to the farm, the family and the field that needed to be seeded was completed in no time at all.

The farmer had noticed after a short amount of time that his own animal was beginning to move about much better. He was healing fairly well. And as this happened, the white horse began to toss his head about and whinny more often as well. It was as if he knew that his visit was just about done.

Once the farmer's animal was fully able to pull the plough again, the white horse left the farm by flying out of the enclosure that held him. I told the old man that I didn't believe that horses could fly. I was then shown a photograph of the horse in flight as he exited the farm that day.

On a later trip back to Ireland, I tried visiting the old man once again who lived down the road and was told he had passed away. I asked the woman in the house if she knew of the horse and its ability to fly. She went to a corner bureau and produced the same picture I was shown on my previous trip to Ireland. I asked her if I could take a picture of her picture and she gave me the original photo. I told her that one day, her husband's story would be in a book that I would write about my trips to Ireland. She wished me and my book project well and sent me off with a wonderful photo and blessing.

But before I left her I asked her again about the horse, her husband and when he first heard the story. She told me that he was the farmer in the story, but that the same event had happened to his father as well. I then asked her when it had happened to his dad. She said she believed it was sometime in the early 1900's.

After the tiny hairs on the back of my neck subsided. I merely squeaked out a meek "thank you" and left quietly pondering that the horse I saw in the 1970's couldn't have been the same animal. Could it?

"The Hungry Dog at Aunt Kathleen's Door"

This story was told to me by an uncle about ten years after it happened. I always loved it because I always loved animals, especially dogs.

A seemingly stray dog had kept coming to the back door of my grandmother's new house. My aunt, her spouse and some of their younger children lived in the house as well. They had all moved into the new house from the old farm in Glenfarne to Manorhamilton. The house was modern with indoor plumbing and several bedrooms that accommodated everybody. My grandmother was terrified to pull the cord in the ceiling in the bathroom thinking that the toilet and its plumbing would explode. She was much older at this time and only knew an outhouse without plumbing of any kind and was just not used to indoor plumbing.

So this new house was very cozy. The even had a garden with year-long flowers that grew around it adding much color and beauty. But they never had any pets. They had always had dogs, chickens, the cow and the donkey but here the house was animal-free.

After the evening meal, my aunt Kathleen would gather all the scraps of food from everyone's plates and bring out to the back of the house. There was a small black and white dog, almost like a border collie, that started coming one day and she would leave food for him. She never knew his name but he was very polite and was always patient and waited for her. He never scratched on the door and from what I was told, he never barked either. He was a grateful little dog and was so much so that one day he showed up at the house with a friend. He brought another little buddy with him to share his food with. My aunt didn't shoo away the other dog either. She fed them both and they both stood there, with tails wagging waiting for her to put the two trays down in front of each of them. She showed them both respect by feeding each one his own tray. Being a dog owner myself, I'm sure they were happy about her doing this.

After they were done eating the border collie would come over to her and nudge her hand. She patted him on the head and he looked up at her. An odd thing she noticed was that he always seemed to give her a wink. First he closed one eye for a moment then blinked both and then went on his way. She had noticed this winking a few times before with him but never recalled seeing a dog do this before.

On some days the dog didn't come so she kept the leftovers for him wrapped up in her refrigerator for the next day. Not too long after the dog didn't show for almost a week and she was missing him. I was told she would stand outside for a considerable amount of time waiting to see if he would show.

After the second week passed, she figured that maybe his owner found him or perhaps somebody took him in. She left one final plate of food for him outside her back door in case he might come during the night.

That same evening after everyone went to bed, my grandmother awoke with a terrible pain in her side. It was quite late and my aunt wasn't sure what to do. She was afraid to get grandma out of bed so she threw an overcoat over her nightgown, woke her husband and told him that they needed to drive up into the town to wake the chemist (pharmacist). As they were backing out of their driveway, aunt Kathleen saw a man crossing the street at the corner of their lot. He too was wearing a long overcoat. He had a hat and seemed to be carrying one of those old fashioned doctor cases. She shouted to him and asked him if he knew the chemist in the town and if it was possible to get something for grandma who was suffering a terrible pain in her side. He mentioned the chemist's name and told my aunt that he had some medication in his bag that might help her.

They pulled the car back into its spot in the driveway and hurried him to the back door of the house. Before entering he told my aunt that he was visiting the town and was a relative of their local chemist. He gave the names of who he knew and that was good enough for my aunt because this was during a time when everyone knew everyone else and trust was a common occurrence.

So he entered the house and was escorted to the back bedroom that belonged to my grandmother. He spoke with her and they exchanged the appropriate information. He then produced the little bottle of pills and gave her what she needed. He left more of the same with my aunt and headed towards the door he came in. She grabbed her purse to compensate him and he waved his hand saying there was no charge. When she insisted he insisted against it again. When they reached the door, she opened it for him and he stepped out. She told him how uncanny it was that he happened to be walking by at the moment they needed a doctor. He merely looked back at her and winked that familiar wink that she had seen so many times with the hungry dog that used to come to her back door.

The "Rush"

My aunt Margaret told me this story when I was a bit older. It was explained to me as if it was something that she wanted me to know about and be aware of.

In W.B. Yeats poem, *"The Hosting of the Sidhe"*, there is an energy present there that my aunt wanted to teach me about. First, I am going to say right out front here that this type of energy is not for the faint of heart. At the age I am now, I am still trying to understand and grasp what it is really all about. All I know at present is that I give my highest level of respect to this energy and honor it with my true self and all that I am.

There is an energy out in the great vast order of things that rescues people when they are in trouble. When a feeling of absolute hopelessness overwhelms a person, a clear mind is given and a solution is shown to that individual. I was somehow pulled out of freezing cold water on the top of a hill with tiny little children to thank. My father was rescued by a woman holding a glowing blue orb or sphere-like object on the banks of the Niagara River. My brother survived going off a cliff into a ravine in Germany. And there are more stories from other family members as well. But my Aunt Margaret seemed to know and understand this "Rush".

"There is much more to it than that," she said to me, sipping her tea.
If I stayed loyal to my projects and kept moving forward with them and did not weaken or give up, the "Rush" would assist me along my way. So, I have remained faithful to my path and remember her with an intense

fondness for educating me about this energy and the knowing that it is always going to be there when needed the most.

I asked her what she knew about the Sidhe (pronounced "she") and she mentioned in a whisper that the older members of my family still believed in them. They are a part of the "Rush" and still exist underground. She then explained to me more of what she believed in and what she was told by my grandmother, her mother, "Mommy-Travers." What I was told then, did not make sense to me at that time but as I got older, it started to and even more so today.

The Man from "Up the Town" and his Little People

There was a man "up the town" as it was put to me, who had a story about The Little People that I just had to hear for myself.

The man who told me the story was elderly at the time. He said that on several occasions he had little tasks to do that he just couldn't finish before sundown. I remembered the old fairy tale of the shoemaker and asked the man if his story was similar. He told me outright, looking into my eyes directly that The Little People did in fact, exist and they were a vital part of his completing his tasks on time.

At first he didn't know how his tasks were getting completed but then one night he heard all kinds of commotion in his barn and tiptoed to see what all the ruckus was. He told me he saw tiny little individuals assembling his lanterns and weaving the straps of leather in the vests that he created for his patrons.

He knew he had to repay them somehow for all their work so he tried to communicate with them to see what they wanted for payment. Through a bizarre understanding between himself and The Little People, it was decided that they wanted him to make them small, round and flat discs out of wood. They had one to show him and he graciously accepted the plan. He got busy the next morning making several of these "Fairy Coins" and surprised The Little People by painting each one. Then he gave each of them a stack of their own. They did now know they were getting so many and were quite pleased with the man. They promised to always be about and assist him with any task at hand that he needed them for.

He did ask what they used the discs for but they would not tell him. All they said was that they had a very important use for them and would not tell him anything further. They could get into serious trouble if they told him. The man respected their wishes and continued to leave them a small pile of the wooden discs on the first day of each month. And by the end of that day, the wooden Fairy Coins were all taken away by The Little People.

SUPERSTITIONS, BELIEFS AND SAMHAIN

I tried to get one of my cousin's to go into a cemetery at night in Ireland. He looked at me as if I was crazy in the head and said, "Oh, we never do a thing like that. The spirits would follow you home."

I stared at him for a long moment and convinced him that the dead are dead and can't possibly hurt us. So he jumped up onto the stone wall and I lifted his dog so he could come with us. Once the dog was over my head, he slipped and fell on top of me. The dog was okay, but I had broken a bone in my nose as well as losing my balance. I fell to the ground with the dog on top of me. It was then I realized that maybe the dead wanted us to stay away. We decided to stay away, for that night anyway.

My grandmother, my mother and most of her siblings were quite superstitious. I was often told what to avoid and how to go about a certain task unless I wanted some ill fate to be put upon me.

My Aunt Margaret was superstitious too. She seemed to have specific rituals for almost everything she did. She did love Samhain though. She asked me once over a chat on the telephone if I was coming to visit at Samhain. (Halloween) My mom had passed away and Aunt Margaret was getting much older and wanted me to come see her and Samhain seemed to be a happy time for her.

I asked her and some of my cousins how they celebrated Halloween/Samhain. One of my cousins said that they cut up plastic, black bags and cover themselves with them. Then they go from door to door to snatch up the goodies left by the folks who leave them there. I guess not too long ago, the old timers were very superstitious and would leave food and drink outside of their doors as an offering to keep away the devil or spirits that walk the night. But as folks got a bit wiser and a bit more daring, they went to those houses, dressed up like those demons and creatures that haunt the night and steal away the food. But nowadays, America has influenced Ireland and some towns hand out candy like we do in the States.

Yet still, some of the older folks, still honor the dead by leaving out their ancestors' favorite meals and beverages so that when the veil between our world and theirs is at its thinnest, the spirits can come through and enjoy the things they had when they were in human form. All Saints Day and All Souls Day is what the Catholics call it now, but back when times were simpler, it was Samhain.

Here are a few interesting Irish tidbits to ponder.

If you pass a piece of straw through a wedding band, you will dream of your future husband or wife.

If you burn a candle and drop the melting wax into a bowl of water, it will form the initial of the name of the man/woman you are going to marry.

Press the wife's wedding band on a stye on your eye for a faster healing time.

Never place shoes on a table. Ever!

Keep your back to the wind.

Passing a young child under the belly of a donkey would cure most childhood diseases.

When seagulls head for land, there will be a storm at sea.

Never throw coins from a ship or boat into the water, you invite a storm.

When you peel an apple and are able to keep the skin in one piece, toss it over your right shoulder. It will form the initial of the man or woman you are going to marry.

A dog wags its tail to the right, when it recognizes its master.

If a cat enters a room full of people, the first person it glances at, will die before all the rest.

Don't leave uncooked eggs on a windowsill.

One of my favorites is, always leave by the same door you come in. If you leave by a different door, you take the tranquility of the house with you when you go.

INFLUENCE OF THE CELTIC GODDESS

In 2010, I had a wild and vivid dream about a woman dressed in green and gold. There was a vibrating white mist around her and she stood in the middle of the room. She held something in her hand that had a long handle with a carving and a design on it.

I woke up, grabbed a pencil and drew the image as best as I could. I brought the drawing to a co-worker friend of mine and told him that I had to absolutely make the object in the drawing. He looked at it, gave a long, "Coool...." and took the drawing home with him. By the end of that week he had it completed.

I don't know why I felt so compelled to have this item made but once it was completed, I stored it away till it was time to use it.

As the months came on and I continued giving my lectures and Celtic presentations in various places, other objects began to come into my life as well. One was given to me by a dear friend who had the item for years and wanted me to have it. Another item was purchased from the internet as I felt drawn to it and didn't know why and the last item came to me as I learned about the sacred meaning behind the ancient use of stone in Ireland.

So I had four tools that came into my life that I was supposed to incorporate within my Irish programs. The dream was about a spear, the item from the internet that called to me was a sword. The "cauldron" or rather, cast iron cooking pot, came from a dear friend, and the stone was given to me from someone who brought it back from a sacred site in

Ireland.

After reading about the Goddess Danu and how she was the Mother Goddess of The Tuatha de Danann, I became very interested in her teachings and the ancient Celtic culture she was a part of. I also became quite interested in other goddesses from the Celtic culture as well. I read about their stories and legends and began to understand the significance of the Spear, the Sword, the Cauldron and the Stone. And I use these tools and explain what I have learned when I present my "Lore of the Celtic Goddess" seminars.

MY JOURNEY CONTINUES...

I've always been interested in the Irish and Celtic culture ever since I learned my parents and family came from Ireland. In the 1980's and early 1990's, I volunteered at The Buffalo Zoo during their special events. One of these events was The Leprechaun Village where all the volunteers dressed in Irish costumes and greeted children and adults as they walked through a make-believe Irish forest, village and town.

This was our "Blarney Stone". When a person touched it, it lit up with green lighting on the inside.

One of the magical stops along the way.

'Tis myself. I was one of their Leprechauns.

I have been entering my front garden in Ken-Ton's annual Garden Tour each year. I invite those who visit, to tie a special ribbon of their choice onto my "Rag Tree" in the front of my house. Over the years, the ribbons have grown and multiplied.

My "Rag Tree."

Rag trees can be seen all over Ireland. There are sacred wells marking sacred sites and people who pass through, tie an article of clothing or a ribbon in exchange for a wish or a prayer that needs to be answered. Some of these sacred spots are dedicated to goddesses that were associated with that particular area. The Goddess Brigid has a few sacred wells named for her and has several Rag Trees as well.

Sacred Well dedicated to Brigid. Her statue can be seen holding her sacred flame.

One of my aunts taught me about the hole stones in Ireland.

If two men wanted to strike a bargain, they would agree to meet at one of the hole-stones. They each put their hands into the hole and grasped each other's hand in the center. The stone bound the agreement between the two so their promise was "set in stone."

When mom and dad said goodbye

I included these two events in this book because I want people to know about what happens when we die.

Both of my parents passed away from year-long bouts with lung cancer. I am not going to go into this on a deep level but the long road of their suffering at the end finally came to rest as they slipped away to a peaceful place.

Dad passed away seven years before mom and when he was dealing with his ordeal, mom and I turned their bedroom into a makeshift hospital room. We had Hospice assisting us and a special adjustable bed brought in to accommodate him.

As he got closer to crossing over to the other side, his body began to shut down. During the last day of his life, when he was mostly in a coma, I sat on the end of his bed and talked to him. I wasn't sure if he could hear me but I heard him as he began to speak. He was saying things that I couldn't understand at first but then I began to hear him say something that sounded like names. He reached out his right hand and began pointing to the end of the bed. Then he moved his hand slightly and pointed to the spot right next to the end of the bed. Then he moved it slightly again. It was as if he was seeing things and counting them. I grabbed a pencil and the back of his pill sheet and began writing down the names I thought I was hearing. I felt compelled to do this.

After he passed away, we notified all of his family as well as those still living in Ireland. His brother came for the wake and funeral. At the wake I brought out that slip of paper that I had written the names on and mentioned them to his brother Eamon. He started to get teary-eyed when I told him. I asked Eamon if he knew the names or recognized them. He told me that those were the names of some of their school chums back in Ireland in Elementary School.

Were his buddies coming for him? Were they there to help him cross over? I never remember my dad mention any of his school buddies or even talk about his younger years at school.

I included this event here because it really did happen. I don't know what dad was really seeing that day but he was aware enough to call out the names when he had been in a sleep-coma like state during all the previous days leading up to this.

My dad died later that same day and was finally at rest.

When my mom crossed over, there was another experience worth mentioning here as well. I thought this over and over and kept this to myself since my mom passed, but now I can finally share this because I want people to be aware of things that are much greater than we are.

Like my dad, my mom had her own long battle with lung cancer. I had to take what I learned with my dad's illness and do the exact same for mom. I changed the bedroom into a hospital room once again. When her time was getting near, strange things began to happen.

During my mom's last three days of life, her body was mostly shut down and she kept slipping in and out of a coma like state. Her breaths were short and there were long spaces between them. I hung on to those breaths, thinking that each one was the last, but praying that it wasn't.

Like a shot, she sat up in bed fully awake after being asleep for nearly three days. She began talking to someone after saying my name out loud. I told her that I was present and tried talking to her. She pointed in the direction of the right hand corner of the ceiling and said she saw four individuals coming in her direction. Even though I could not see them myself, I told her that I did see them since she had a smile on her face. They must have been familiar beings due to the expression I remember seeing that day. She lost four siblings in one year, all close to each other and I wondered if perhaps they were her brothers and sisters coming to be there for her passing.

A moment later she reached out her other arm to the side of the bed and said the name, "Annie". Annie was my mom's youngest and favorite sister. She died before all the rest at a young age.

As this was going on and mom was still talking, I decided to get my little portable tape recorder because I didn't want to miss the conversations she was having with her relatives. Plus, I also wanted to remember the peaceful state my mom was beginning to enter. I thought that maybe by recording what I was hearing, I could somehow keep mom alive and not have to let her go. I kept talking to her and telling her that her family was there and it was okay for her to go. I also kept telling her that I was going to be okay and she didn't have to stay and worry about me. I was really hurting so bad on the inside but did all I could to keep it hidden, to stay as calm as I could so that she could finally let go.

The very last person she talked to was her own mother. I know this because mom called out to her as if "Mommy-Travers" was standing right there, next to her bed. I heard my mom say, *"Mommy"*. Within the hour my mom was gone.

And here's the part I hesitate to write, but I have to include this because it is the energy of the amazing powerful transition that has made me quite humble.

I tucked away the tape I recorded of mom and me and her talking to her siblings and her mother. Due to my severe depression of trying to deal with her passing, I could not and did not want to listen to it any time soon.

But a few years ago, I mustered up enough guts to give it a try. I plugged in my tape recorder and retrieved the tape from its hiding place. First I heard my own voice, as I remember it, talking to mom and telling her it was okay for her to go. Then there was a long pause. Then I heard my own voice again telling my mom that grandma was indeed present and that mom was really seeing her. There was "white noise" instead of my mom's voice and then my own voice was heard again. Each time my mom would speak, it was replaced with that static-like white noise. My voice was as clear as if it was being heard in real time. My mom's conversations with her siblings as well as her own mother cannot be heard at all and I know for absolute sure that she was talking to someone just hours before she passed.

When she finally did go, her bedroom lit up with golden light. It wasn't a normal kind of light but rather a soft glowing kind of brightness. I also saw this outside her bedroom window, but I couldn't have because it was an evening in December and it should have been dark outside. It only lasted a few seconds and then she was gone and the glow as well.

I am grateful to my wonderful Irish parents for giving me a childhood filled with wonder and interesting experiences. As of the writing of this book I am back living in the house I grew up in due to the fact that I moved back home to take care of mom when she was terminal. It was rough going for a bit, but the suffering is over and I move on ahead.

I wrote this book in honor of my parents and their quirky, Irish ways. Their humor and stories will always be with me as I continue to remember them with fondness. The Irish lectures, presentations and workshops are performed in their honor as I keep their traditions and beliefs alive for as long as I am able.

I got married in August of 1999. My husband respects the idea of what I am trying to accomplish by preserving my own family's heritage and such and I am grateful to him for his understanding.

**The author and her other half,
Mark DiPasquale.**

Like my ancestors who always had a dog or two, we have adopted a few of our own over the years.

Shadow and Pepper. Always in our hearts. Plus......

Mr. Toby, Miss Bella, Miss Bran-Cear (aka Brandy)

And one final mention here. Two weeks after my mother died, I was walking up my driveway, pondering my thoughts and sadness while missing them. I started talking to them in my head.

"Mom and dad, what should I do with my life now that both of you are gone? I feel lost and unsure of what to do next."

I paused in my driveway and looked toward the sky. I gasped as I saw the clouds part and I stood there wondering how fast I could get my camera. Please know that the image following this was even more precise than the one included here. I got the camera as fast as I could. Feel free to decide for yourself what you see in this picture, but what I saw was a silhouette of Ireland. That's how I knew what to do with the rest of my life. Thank you mom and dad!

ABOUT THE AUTHOR

Eileen A. Canning was born in Lackawanna, New York. She was adopted from Father Baker's. Adopted at an early age, she grew up with two wonderful parents from the west coast of Ireland. She received a teaching degree from Buffalo State College in 1995. She has adopted several animals from a local shelter and strives to give them the best home she possibly can. She continues to teach her Celtic themed workshops and share her stories in order to keep the Celtic traditions alive.

Made in the USA
Middletown, DE
25 August 2015